AF251625

RUMI
A NEW COLLECTION

AF251625

RUMI

A New Collection

Translated from the Persian by

Farrukh Dhondy

GLOBAL COLLECTIVE PUBLISHERS

Published by Global Collective Publishers, LLC
16 North Bryn Mawr Ave., # 1355
Bryn Mawr, Pennsylvania 19010, U.S.A.
www.globalcollectivepublishers.com

First published in India in 2020 by Perennial

Copyright © Farrukh Dhondy, 2022
English translation copyright © Farrukh Dhondy 2022

Print ISBN: 978-1-954021-23-5
eBook ISBN: 978-1-954021-03-7

Farrukh Dhondy asserts the moral right to be
identified as the author of this work.

All rights reserved. No part of this publication may be
reproduced, stored in a retrieval system, or transmitted, in any
form or by any means, electronic, mechanical, photocopying,
recording or otherwise, without the prior permission of the publishers.

Dedication

To Firdaus Ali
Scholar, Translator, and Friend

Contents

The Verses

Lovers think they are searching for the one
Still wondering when wandering will be done
There is only one search beneath the sky
That of the love that merges You and I
And all our books are both the Truth and Lie.

Issah himself was the miracle on earth
The miracle was not the second birth
For Lazarus — or water turned to wine
Issah himself was the timeless divine
Presence that confounded the fear of time–
Him I would follow, the prophet sublime!

O mortal you can look back to the past
The Present being nothing but the last
Sensations of which your mind was aware
The Future is a void, there's nothing there!

Within infliction lurks the remedy
Within Winter the Summer that's to be.
Death resides in the foetus at its birth
All right and wrong are compounds of
this earth

This missing one, the mystery resides
In spaces where the outsides are insides.

The worm whose appetite is for vine leaves
Will suddenly sprout wings as he conceives
That he is not a crawler any more
He is transformed. The sky's an open door

And he's the vine and all the vineyard too.
God's embrace is the same for me and you
Thus, realisation is what it takes
To become yourself when your soul awakes.

Love without a beloved is most pure
And toil without a purpose will endure.

With clever tricks you did the world enthrall
– Giving up tricks was cleverest of all!

Stay awake at night and then greet the dawn
As the moon does, whitening towards morn.

Be the pail of water drawn from the dark
Well - knowing that into light you'll embark.

Dance when the bowl of soul is shattered
Dance when you've nudged the blindfold off
Dance when the battle was all that mattered
Dance though the world stands by to scoff!

When you speak
You make me dumb
Watching your movements
Makes me numb
I fled from your charms
To the shades of my heart
You made my heart a trap
Now we are never apart!

You are both the mirror
And your reflection,
In every moment
The taste and confection
Of eternity exists.

You are both the pain
And the remedy that cures it
You are both the sweet water
And the jug that pours it.

When I first heard a love story
I felt you were somehow in it
I didn't finally find you
– You were with me from that minute

Respect those who resolve
To never tell a lie
Whose egos then dissolve
With His will to comply!

It was only your perfection
That taught me to love
It was from your beauty
I learnt poetry and song
Then I saw you dance
Like celestial spheres above
And thinking only of you
I now dance all night long.

MEDIUMS

A story is a medium
With a moral aftermath
As water is a medium
Carrying warmth to a bath

– and a message from the fire to your skin

Only few can endure fire
And none are intrepid
We daren't challenge the flames
As prophet Ibrahim did

– and like the salamander he went in

Your feeling free from hunger
Depends on how much bread
Or other nourishment
On which your hunger fed

– you know you will be hungry once again

Do we appreciate beauty
It's always around us
Or can we only see it
When rose gardens surround us?

— does beauty assail all women and men?

Your body is a shield
That partially reveals
The burning flame inside you
And the passion it conceals

— all love aspires to draw the veil aside

Stories, water, your body
Are mediums that can hide
The spirit which is the essence
The flame that burns inside

— and veils are made of vanity and pride

So contemplate the medium.
Confident it will show
A glimpse of the secret
We fragmentarily know.

TO THE MOON

O moon shine down upon us,
Don't sleep, we need your light.

And circle in the heavens
Illuminating night.

O stay awake, lamp of the world
Gold stone of the sky that God has hurled.

Is solitude more precious than
Fathomless company?

Is power over a nation
Better than to be free?

If in your confined room
You spend your time alone
You can study the imprint
Of the value that you own.

Candles exist to disappear in flame
And becoming nothing, cast no shadow.
They are but tongues of light. Aren't we the
same?

Regard the dwindling candle as a life
Coming to its end free of pride and shame,
Free from virtue, from vice and human strife.

The sun is love
And lovers the specks of dust
Which around it circulate.

The wind is life
And the trees it sways the dancers
Who to its songs gestate.

The greatest love, O Sufi
Is love without a lover.

The most productive toil
Is without purpose to its endeavour.

Only fools deceive themselves
Thinking they're cunning and clever.

The cleverest trick my friend
Is to abandon tricks forever.

No melody is hidden from The King
Not even those in thought which you
don't sing.

All poets want to sell their every word
I serve Him whose verses are never heard.

I was shy and hid my face
You made me sing, I lost all trace

Of modesty. And now no sign
Remains of it, I shout for wine!

I tried to pose as dignified
While sitting on my mat to pray

Now children gather round me
To include me in their play

WHY FEAR DEATH
(from *Ariosto*)

Starting life as a grain of dust I died
And passed into the life of moving things
Which in turn became creatures of the tide
And crawled to earth and to the air with wings

Then these creatures gave way to humankind.
Death is the stepping stone to higher states
So, one day I shall die and hope I find
Myself admitted through heavenly gates

Where angels dwell and in time also die.
And thus, transformed, I'll shed angelic shape
And become that which neither brain nor eye
Can imagine or see. This last escape

To non-being where forms do not exist
United with His single cosmic mist.

SEED MARKET

Where is this place of trade
In which incredible bargains are made?

Where a single rose can buy
Rose gardens which multiply

And a single seed bought possesses
Infinite wildernesses?

Where a single breath inhaled with ease
Contains within it the Divine breeze?

O Mortal, who fear turning to dust
Or winding in air as ashes must

Think – you are but a tear which
Consciousness keeps
Sequestered from the eternal ocean's deeps

From whence we all come, as drops of sorrow
Separated from the Deep because Life
must borrow

Droplets to fashion worlds from eternity
And only to Return is finally To Be!
O mortal, cast all pride aside
Embrace the ocean, the eternal tide.

Abandon your puerile resistance
To embrace the real gift of existence

– A proud falcon has landed upon your shoulder
The reason it has is in the mind of the beholder.

I bowed to him who set the world on fire
Flaying me in all-consuming desire
The flames around me lapped and stretched and licked
Around my selfish ego's funeral pyre

The engulfing flames were a loving cure
To burn your ego in love will ensure
Your union with the Beloved who said
"This pain without a word or sigh endure!"

I observe flowers blooming every night
The blossoms of the sky, these recondite
Flames burning without heat unlike the sun
The lanterns of space and time infinite

These breaths from their inspiration arise
My heart once cold is warmed by flaming sighs
The stars are lights of love – he tells me – so
That anyone can see them in the skies

The fragrance dances on the morning breeze
Is it rose or musk sent to me to tease
My senses from my true love's garden wild
These perfumes that can both disturb and
please?

Before our puny lives all go to hell
Arise, obey the summons of the bell
The caravan will carry her far away
And with her all that fragrance? – Who
can tell?

TRUTH AND FALSITY

Let us not say that any doctrine lies.
The scent of truth ensnares the minds of men;
A gem of truth from every doctrine cries
Out to be heard from every untruth's den.

Truth is the light of dark within the night,
Testing its power to shine through the dark
The discernment in all that's wrong, of right
Challenging truths from untruths to embark.

In ragged crowds the fakir goes unseen;
His rags are the dress of humility.
Learn to discern the pure from the unclean
The spiritual Prince from earthly Royalty.

The traders of this world trade merchandise
Buying the good and rejecting the bad.
If these were both the same the enterprise
Of any distinction, could not be had.

Between right and wrong there's no equality.
The Sandalwood tree stands out from the Yew.
Only a fool says there's no falsity
Only a scoundrel says nothing is true!

ALL RELIGIONS ARE ONE

When the righteous regardless of faith
Invoke the prophets who direct a soul
To Him, they are like wine from several cups
Poured to mingle and fill a single bowl.

Their praises are directed to The One
So all prayers and religions are the same
Directed ultimately to one light
Of Him regardless of the earthly name

That one or other religion may use
To praise The One. Though some in error fall
Into mistaking the radiance of light
From the Moon reflected on a blank wall

For the light from the radiant moon itself.
Or seeing its reflection in a well
They mistake its image for the real thing
And worship it. Only the Moon can tell

If this worship, being for a reflection,
Is idolatory leading prayers astray –
Are all images condemned as idols
Forbidden to the worshipful who pray?

TODAY

Today I drink in taverns of the soul
Today all abandonment is my goal
Today don't ask me what we drunkards drink
Today just fill the cup and smile, don't think!
Today no night of separation looms
Today the brides will unite with their grooms
Today we celebrate with Saki's song
Today with jugs and cups the night is long
Today the light of day becomes the night
Today all time suffers a mental blight
Today it's celebration, song and wine
Today is blessed with the spirit divine
Today we drown in what the Saki gives
Today the brightest Sun of Tabriz lives
Today Shams of Tabriz makes us all see
That all is oneness! Stuff philosophy!

THE HOUSE OF LOVE
(Ghazal 332 from *Diwan-e-Shams*)

Why is there always music in the air?
Ask only this of The One who lives there.

Why are there idols in the House of God?
Magian temples lit by him? That's odd!

What priceless treasure should the
world applaud?
The claimant owner is a cheat and fraud.

Don't dare attack this house, leave it alone.
Its owner is drunk every night and prone

To ecstasies divine. This house was meant,
With every chamber blessed with holy scent

And every door and hinge of it that creaks
With sounds divine and tuneful verses speaks.

To be the home of that singular one
Who inherits the gift of Solomon.

Sufi, we who await his Divine grace
Ask of Him, when he will show us his face

That gazing on it we might be set free
From this deceitful world of fantasy?

The garden confuses blossom and leaf
And baited birds don't recognize the thief.

The master of the planets and the moon
The beauty that causes the heart to swoon

Zuleikha's maids on seeing Joseph's charm
Contemplated the fate of their self-harm.

So, enter this abode where all must drink
With wine of the divine and the instinct

Which tells you that to linger at the door
Is to remain in darkness evermore.

So have no fear of the lion's lair
With faith in your own courage enter there.

All thought conspires to lock the seeker out
Of His house, so relieve yourself of doubt

And let your tongue only pronounce his name
As idle words can set His house aflame.

GHAZAL 1919 (From *Masnavi*)

One definition of love is to fly
Up to the heavens tearing every veil
To breathe and at the first breath to deny
That breathing is to love of no avail

And taking a first step without your feet
Which only confuse advance with retreat

To see only the truth and not the eye
Which is the chief instrument of the lie.

I spoke to my heart saying, "We have won
Entrance into the circles of the heart
And did this Breath come only from The One
And from what or whom did this
throbbing start?

So, speak, O bird, the language of the air.
It's a music which I can interpret."
The soul in flight says it has no regret.
"Witnessing His creation, I was there

When He in heaven's workshop worked away
Creating the world with water and clay
And though I tried to make good my escape
They dragged me back to give my spirit shape."

GHAZAL 2523

O heart of mine, o worshipper of flame
Who will conspire now to quell this fire?

O Saki, I am burning, pour a draught
Is it from heaven or from hell this fire?

Beautiful one, that night you came to me
And with your charms you did compel this fire.

O Cupbearer you soothed my heart with wine
Through cooling kisses what befell this fire?

You took me captive to a secret house
And poured your sweetness to repel this fire.

You offered me a choice of flame or gold
Though either choice would not repel the fire.

So, Rumi rise out of Shams-u-Tabrez
And flee into the gold to swell the fire.

ULTIMATE LIGHT

Put reason away and let sleep descend
The sleep of mad illogic which can lend
Oblivion of night and day which can blend
Into visions that madness can defend.

Day and night both exist because this earth
Rotates, but for this madman there's no birth
Of sunrises, for what the madman sees
Is time and space as dazzling panoplies.

In pursuit of this madness you become
A bird, a fowl, a fish or even some
Friend of that same oblivion which will keep
His madness in suspension while you sleep.

So, sleepwalker embrace The One entranced
Who loosened his curly tresses and danced
To enrich with the evidence of soul
And to the realm of madness to enroll

You and me from consciousness which is blight
To Shams of Tabriz, the Ultimate Light.

SINCE YOU WENT

You left me – and left me crying
But this you know
The thirst for you can't be quenched by trying
But this you know

Your love entered my heart and settled there
But this you know
Turning this haven into a nest of care

The rose withered; nightingales flew away
Leaving me painful thorns, darkening my day

My cries of pain turned falcons into owls
And turned proud mountain birds into
cheap fowls

Like pomegranates I sweetened your lips
Now I'm a burnt-out flame, the dark eclipse

The secret of your love is in my heart
But this you know since we have been apart

Shams-u-Tabriz was ever the sweetest fruit
That led me to this martyrdom's pursuit

I AM YOU

I am the dust that's dancing in the light
I am the sun whose rays destroy the night

I beseech the dust particles to stay
I beg the sun to procreate the day

I am the enveloping morning mist
I am the twilight which the sunset kissed

I am the wind that shakes the tops of trees
I am the surf that rides all seven seas

I am the mast, the rudder and the deck
I am the coral reef, its final wreck

I am the tree with squawking parakeets
I am the sound of silence in the streets

I am the music coming through the flute
I am the flint and metal in pursuit

Of the spark that initiates all fire
Compelling moths to their fatal desire

I am the rose, its fragrance and its thorn
And the nightingale within song reborn

I am all orders of beings that are
All galaxies, all space, the Evening Star

I am what is and isn't' I am who?
I know that You, who know,
Know I am You.

I CAME ALIVE
(Ghazal 1393)

I was once dead
But then I came alive
I once was full of tears
Now laughing, I survive.

Only when Love came to me
And embraced me in its Whole
My eye was full of visions
And everlasting my soul.

Now my heart is like a lion's
And like Venus I shine bright.
Love said, "Take on this madness
Or get out of my sight!"

Love offered me its nectar
Insisting I must be drunk;
I drank in Love's wide tavern
And was ecstatically sunk.

Surrendering to oblivion
I became an obedient tool
Drowning in Love's proud splendour
I became rejoicing's fool.

Love said I was a candle,
A light for the gathered folk.
Unaware of any brightness
I felt was scattered smoke.

Love called me a Sheikh and leader
And said I was the guide who'd pave
The path of love for all others;
I protested I was His slave.

He said, "You already have feathers
And can fly on your sprouted wings
And so, I don't need to gift you these!"
How could I say I had none of these things?

This New Love as it came to my heart
Said, "I shall descend like rain
In grace and generosity
I'll relieve you of human pain."

Old Love whispered a persuasion,
Urging I stay close to her breast.
I promised her I'd obey her wish,
Her presence was where I'd rest.

The fountain of light that is the sun
Casts shadows on earth of the willow;
When love's shaft struck my heart and head
I swooned and succumbed to the blow.

Love set this heart and soul aglow,
My heart was consumed by its magic.
It cast off its ragged garments
And began to weave a silk fabric.

Love transformed me from a swaggering
Slave, ass-driver and lowly thief
Into a generous, selfless being,
A king, a lord and chief.

The sugar of Love brought me sweetness.
I reside in its embrace.
The earth gives thanks for the arching sky
And the light that descends from space.

Beyond the seven layers of heaven
We become the shining stars.
I was Venus and am now the moon
And all heaven's brightness is ours.

When Yusuf emerged from the waters
Of the well, his beauty shone through;
Dissolve in that well, O Sufi,
Yusuf's beauty is me and you!

Move silently on this chessboard,
Your powers by Him prescribed;
Destined to be happy and blissful
Once your vanity and ego have died.

THE CAGED SELF

O bird in the cage with your untried wings
Don't envy the desert's free bird who sings.

Don't crawl like salamanders into fire
Or embrace its suicidal desire.

O Tailor these smithies are not for you
Hammers on anvils are not things you do.

If you're not water, don't enter the sea
Though all rivers which flow cause you envy.

And if on a ship caught up in a storm
Make sure as a survivor you perform

The actions that will keep you safe from harm
Holding the stern tight till the sea is calm.

All access to heaven is through The One
Called Issah, who some say was Allah's son.

The young fruit can but ripen on the tree
And grow till it reaches maturity.

Just so, Shams-u-Tabriz is apprenticed
To That Ultimate whose feet must be kissed.

MYSTIC ODE 833
Eternal Light

We are wedded to eternity
When our lives are done
There remains no mystery
We dissolve into The One.

The rays of sunlight scatter
Forming the shadows' shapes
Multiplicities of matter
Are gathered in a bunch of grapes.

Death is but an illusion
So surrender your mortal soul
And subject it then to fusion
Of the fragment with the whole.

HE exists beyond good and bad
No judgement can apply
Beyond all feeling, not happy nor sad
Beyond the realms of Truth and Lie.

Fix your eyes on the Eternal Face
With no idle talk of invisibility.
Surrender to Him and He will place
That in your eye which you must see.

And look! The bird of vision in flight
Alights upon your inner eye
To shine with God's Eternal Light
On wings of desire this bird does fly.

WE ARE BUT WATER AND CLAY

We are but copies of the heaven's shapes
Made perishingly of water and clay
The originals of heaven endure
Their earthly replicas must fade away.

Don't weigh your hearts and mind with
thoughts of death
All beauty that enchants the eye and ear
All landscapes, art and inventions of life
Must perish – Yet not in the way you fear!

The streams and fountains spring and overflow;
No stream or brook or spring forever dies.
This mortal fear of oblivion is vain
Existence is eternity's disguise.

This fountain is the portrait of the soul
From which the world and all created things

Emanate. It can never cease to flow
Fed by the waters of eternal springs.

So, Sufi be assured that you may drink
And let your thirsting heart be quenched and rest.
All those who deem this fountain dry may fret
Till the force of its waters manifest

Themselves and carry cynics on their tide.
The moment that creation reached the earth,
A ladder was placed for rude clay to climb
From mineral to plants which then gave birth

To animals and finally to Man,
With knowledge, reason, faith, God's miracle
To give the particles of dust such life
His proud creation and the pinnacle

On earth – and yet through life destined to go
To the realm of angels who never die
But are as drops in the eternal sea
–From one drop seven oceans multiply.

They called the blessed Issah 'Son of God'
Though God is indivisible: The Truth
Though you in body grow withered and old
In Him you have assured immortal youth.

THE HARPIST

A harpist who through all his confined youth
Had flattered the known world on dulcet
strings
Realised that Time imposes its truth
And that the charms of youth had taken wings

And flown into the unforgiving past
And that his gift of charm, his instrument
Had weathered and had several broken strings.
No prayer of his could force Time to relent.

The harpist went to Medina in hope
And prostrate in the holy places prayed
Not for his past or youth to be restored
But that his broken harp should be remade

Into the plangent instrument it was
And though old age had changed his
singing voice

His fingers hadn't lost the skill to play
His restored harp. He swore that he'd rejoice

And uttering this prayer he placed the harp
Upon a sacred grave and laid his head
Using it as pillow. Very soon
His soul departed. The harpist was dead.

His soul then sped to the timeless region
Out of our known three-dimensional space
Free now of all material wants and grief
Free even of the need for divine grace.

He had no head, no heart, no memory
No fears, worries nor needs no outstretched hand
To gather rose or herbs or basil leaves
A free soul's joy mortals can't understand

The joy Job felt when healed in the fountain.
He went to the pure realm which has no door
No lock or key for human will to open
And there the harpist lay for evermore

Silent now as his melodious harp.
But Caliph Omar heard a voice while sleeping
Saying. 'Give that dead harpist gold dinars -
It should be seven hundred for his keeping
That he may wake and buy new silken strings
And play the harp again for all the world.'
Omar was startled by the voice and went
To the graveyard to find the harpist curled

In deathly bliss upon a holy grave.
Omar approaching, sneezed. The harpist stirred
Miraculously to full consciousness
And Omar repeated the words he'd heard.

'Take dinars to the harpist. He'll awake
And give them to him so he can repair
The magic harp and music again.'
The harpist bewildered began to stare

At Caliph Omar. And then picking up
His gold harp he dashed it into pieces.
"These songs have held me captive breath by
breath
A naive fool. Destruction now releases

Me from the sexy rhythms of Iran
And the classic melodies of Iraq.
These verses kept me warbling like a dove
Or chirping like a nightingale or lark

I now surrender this imprisonment
Inside the self that vainly says, 'I am!'
Then Omar turned to the harpist and said
'This selflessness is but another sham.

You are held captive in freedom's embrace
A prisoner of that very freedom's quest.
Seek nothing but the hollow of the reed
And put your beating restless heart to rest!

Seek only that which is beyond seeking.
Drown yourself in the radiance of The Lord.
The self you seek to free is an illusion
And this drowning is your first step toward

The Joyous annihilation of that self'
So, hearing this the harpist cast aside
The disciplines of our earthly music
Abandoning harmonies that divide.

ISSAH IN FLIGHT

Issah, the son of Mariam, was in flight
As though possessed of unshakeable fright
When a believer in his truth seeing
Him thus asked Jesus from what he was fleeing

But Issah made no answer, running still
As though his flight was fulfilling the will
Of some higher purpose. His pursuer
Asked Him, 'Aren't you the one I thought you
were –

The Nazarene who could awake the dead
And feed a multitude with fish and bread
Then surely nothing can fill you with fear.'
Then Issah said these words for all to hear

'I pronounce His Name to the lame and blind
That they may leave their affliction behind.
His sacred word turns water into wine
To bring you hope and faith in the Divine.

But there are those who will not heed the word.
They're like the rock that remains undeterred
By gentle rain that falls from heaven above
Unaffected by all His cleansing love.

These foolish creatures don't know wrong
from right;
From that foolishness have I taken flight.

Atoms of water from the oceans rise.
Before the heat of conceit, reason dries
Up - so Issah's flight is a metaphor,
A parable that's laid at reason's door.

THE GARMMARIAN AND THE
BOATMAN

A grammarian needing to get across
A wide river hired himself a boat
Directing the boatmen to a remote
Destination. Then being at a loss

For intellectual stimulus he turned
To the young handsome boatman as he rowed
And extracting some book of grammar showed
The boatman a theorem he'd discerned

Of great grammatical complexity
Asking the young man what grammar he knew.
"Sir, I know nothing beyond two and two
Make four!" the boatman said quite brazenly.

"Then you've lived only half a life young man,"
The grammarian said in his haughty way.
And as he said this, clouds darkened the day
And in the waters a whirlpool began

To stir the river and threaten the boat.
The boatman with a smile turned to him.
'So philosopher, I hope you can swim –
The chance we'll get to shore is now remote.'

'Of course, I can't,' the pompous man replied.
'Then you've wasted not half but all your life,'
The boatman said. No intellectual strife
Will save you from the rising of the tide.

Obliteration of the self will prove
Solution in dissolution. Your mind
Reflecting grammar and logic will find
It cannot grasp how worlds and times do move.

THE MERCHANT AND THE
PARROT

A merchant kept a parrot in a cage
A squawking, talking bird who was
quite a sage,

A beautifully-feathered cockatoo
Who spoke in several languages he knew.

This merchant planned a trip to travel East
To Hindustan, and feeling that the least

He could do for his servants was enquire
What gift from Hind did each of them desire?

And asking this, he asked his parrot too
'What can I bring you, blessed cockatoo?'

The parrot said, "The best gift you can give
Me is tell the parrots there how I live.

Inside a metal prison, that's my space
Isolated from the rest of the avian race.

Tell them that I spend all my life longing to see
The likes of them, as I've never had company.

Ask them if it's my fate that I have grown
To live and, I guess, then to die alone?

And ask them if it's right that they are free
To tour the skies and flit from branch to tree

While I, their cousin, languish behind bars
While they peck fruit and breathe the scent of
flowers?

Brother and sister parrots think of me
And raise a curse against captivity.'

This parrot then recalled Lyla-Majnun
Whose tragic tale entailed separation too.

Then addressing the Merchant, the bird said,
'The servants of each Master lie in dread

Of dismissal for disobedience –
A fear of which you Masters have no sense.'

Now suppose, gentle reader, through this tale
A deeper sense and meaning were to prevail

And further that this story as a whole
Has cast a parrot as a metaphor for soul

Which when caught in the Ecstasy of Grace
Perceives His opposites-embracing Face

In which reflection good and bad are one
And darkness is the brightness of the sun.

His cruelty and everything that's wrong
Are right and gentle as the harp-string's song

And death and every funeral's sad dirge
Sounds like the joyous songs when brides
emerge

From veils. His Violence and Grace, though
extremes
Are but one. It's only what it seems.

Our forms are worldly, our souls are in No
Place
Which is the realm no intelligence can trace.

Now, leaving behind argument's metaphor
Let's return to our narrative and explore

The story of the Merchant to whom his bird
Bequeathed a strong request as you have heard.

This merchant on reaching Hindustan's plains
Kept both eyes and ears open to catch strains

Of a pandemonium of parrots and soon found
A flock by a woodland pecking on the ground.

He began to deliver the message word for word
And as he did, he saw this single bird

Who was perched in front of him begin to shake
And ripple like waters of a stormy lake.

The birds around her flapped and squawked
and cried
But she turned over, closed her eyes and died.

The merchant was dismayed and at what he'd
done
Was her spirit and his own bird's spirit One?

Like iron on stone had his words become
the spark
That lit a fatal flame, both negative and dark

As death? So, traveller treading in a field
Of cotton be circumspect - do not yield

To temptation to set the cotton on fire
With words, like deadly sparks. Control
your desire

To spread the plague of injurious words
Though they reflect the cries of
imprisoned birds.

Know now it's Issah's breath that constitutes
each soul.
One breath wounds, the other makes whole.

It's only the veil of illusion which conspires
To distort, so when it's lifted, we'd all speak
like Messiahs.

THE WOLF THE FOX AND THE LION

A fox, a wolf and lion all agree
That one or two are always less than three;

They'll form a trio and hunt for some prey.
With such a team, what can come in their way?

They'd share their skills so creatures big
and small
Could not escape – they'd stalk and bag
them all.

The lion felt a certain misgiving.
What was he doing with these? Wasn't he
the King?

And having teamed up with this lowly pair
Was that stupid and a cause for despair?

Probably not! The moon outshines the stars
And chaff is weighed in scale where golden bars

Are also measured but not deemed the same,
The Lion thought. "So, I can hunt for game

With these fellows. The Prophet had his four
Apostles and no-one thought they were more

Than followers." The Lion was content
And so, with his two companions he went

To the mountains and soon they bagged a hare,
An Ox, a goat, a wild boar and a pair

Of mountain antelopes. They dragged
them back
To the forest leaving blood on the track.

The fox and wolf kept thinking of their share;
Now with their catch would the Lion be fair?

The Lion was the jungles' royalty
The guardian of all justice so would he

Condescend to give each of them a third?
The Lion was aware as though he'd heard

These creatures voicing their concerns aloud.
As the King of Justice, he was endowed

With the gift of detecting every thought
Whether it be benevolent or fraught

So evil thoughts can never be concealed.
The scavenging pair's thoughts were
thus revealed

To the Lion who kept a smiling face
Though he thought their demands were
a disgrace.

Were they not satisfied that he'd allowed
These two scoundrels to stand out from
the crowd

And go along with him for company?
How dare they demand a share guarantee?

How can you in conscience seek to defy
The giver of the gift to beautify

This world. Can a painting evaluate
The painter and the skill which did create

It? So, creature, put all thoughts of gain away.
Measuring your worth leads you to dismay.

And with these thoughts the Lion beamed
a smile
To disguise his perception and beguile

These scoundrels who had dared to match
their worth
Against their King. So, creatures of this earth

Beware God's smiles are deceptions which test
Our greed and lust; his smile is the bequest

Of this world's riches. Like the Lion's grin
It is a trap so don't be taken in.

The Lion now asked the wolf to divide
The catch between the hunters and decide

Who should get what? Should all three
have a share?
"You Majesty, my judgement is the hare

Being the smallest should go to the fox
And you My Lord, of course deserve the ox.

As for the goat and deer I am content
To keep them as my share with your consent."

"What do you mean, dear wolf, by 'you'
and 'me'?
We went on the hunt as one entity.

When you are in my presence, we are one;
The light of day is nothing but the Sun

And so, dissolve yourself," the Lion said
"Without my essence, every self is dead.

Nothing exists except the Divine face
Deny all 'self' and vanity, embrace

Him and the vast and Divine melting pot.
Salvation is where 'I' and 'we' are not.

DALKAQ

The King of Timid made it known
That he required a messenger
To deliver to Samarkand
A secret message he alone
Would share with his ambassador

Who should, he said, go and return
In five days from his setting out
On horseback or in caravan
And any volunteer would earn
More gold than he could dream about.

The King's jester was called Dalkaq
And was not at the time at court
But out of town when word reached him.
So he borrowed a horse and hurried back
To deliver a sapient thought

To his Lord. Though arriving late
He sought an audience with the King.
"What could this clown want at this hour?
Surely this fool's wisdom can wait,
Or is it some urgent pressing thing?"

When asked a question Dalkaq would
Raise a finger to his face
As though he needed time to think
— The King and courtiers understood
The function of this moment's grace —

Allowing Dalkaq at such times
To come up with some witty line,
A joke, an aphoristic phrase,
Some pithy or outrageous rhymes
Or a parable involving a concubine.

But on this night Dalkaq had paused
With that raised finger much too long.
Had he brought news of treachery
Or other betrayal – what had caused
This pregnant silence, what was wrong?

Then in time our jester spoke
Saying he'd heard the King's demand
For a volunteer courier to convey
For gold and honours beyond a joke
Some Royal message to Samarkand.

The King replied, "Yes clown, it's true
I need a messenger I can trust!"
"Well," said Dalkaq, "I came in haste
To assure you Majesty I can't do
Any of this, so I think you must

Find someone else to ride north-east;
I lack the stamina and wit."
The King was outraged hearing this
"Is this a joke, you ungrateful beast?
Why wake me to say you won't do it?"

"That's like the family of a bride
Who from the groom's house has no word
Where they prepare a wedding feast
A secret from the bride they hide
A secret never to be heard?"

The lesson friends, is like Dalkaq
Some pretend to be on the Path
Of selflessness to meet The Friend;
-Infinite light beyond the dark,
Annihilated ego's aftermath. . . . .

THE ETERNAL ARGUMENT

An Arab Bedouin's wife would every day
Give him a hearty earful; she would say:

"All our neighbours are happy except us!"
Her husband turned a deaf ear to this fuss

Though she'd complain about the dearth
of bread.
"What do you expect we can eat instead?

We have no utensils, no water jug
We drink from our cupped palms - we have no
mug.

I have no clothes. I live my life in tatters.
You pay no heed to these essential matters

We have no blankets; we freeze when it's cold.
Before my time you forced me to grow old.

The only cake I've seen is the full moon
Imagining its flavour, like some loon.

And when I point this out you get annoyed
–Our tribe treats us as beggars to avoid.

All Arab men are supposed to be brave
Providers—it's not luxury I crave

But just the bare minimum in this life
I might as well have been a corpse's wife!

Ten years I've lived with you and come to this!"
He regarded her brief silences as bliss.

But shortly this poor wife would start again
And disturb the ether perhaps in vain

Complaining about God and saying He
Was trusted to treat humans benignly

Bestowing bounty with the proviso
That it would be granted — but tomorrow!

"The idiot to such deception succumbs
The wise one knows 'tomorrow' never comes."

The husband would insistently reply,
"The currents of our lives are flowing by;

You complain about money constantly,
An obsession that means you can't be free.

Just think how free the thoughtless creatures
live
Assuming each day that Nature will give

Them what they need. The nightingales all sing
Their thanks to God. And all other living

Beings from elephants to tiny gnats
Are confident of nourishment and that's

What the bounty of God is all about.
It's greedy pigs like you who rant and shout

Not realising that life's experience
Is the prompting of His holy essence

To tell us we were once the healthy vine
And demonstrate that though we must decline

If we give way to discontent and greed
You are one with me, we two must succeed

In being like the perfect pair of shoes
If one is tight, disparity ensues.

The well-matched door with its opposite locks.
The Lion never mates with Wolf or Fox."

His wife, unimpressed by these similes,
Would interrupt saying, "Hang on a minute,
please –

You're happy to be poor you hypocrite,
This pretence of humility is shit!

You scramble after bones like some stray dog.
Your metaphors are blind men in a fog.

You're not as satisfied as you pretend
= And don't call me your wife, I want to end

This misery. I made a grave mistake
I n marrying you. You think you are the snake

Charmer, but you are just the snake who
charms
Or tries to beguile listeners with your psalms

And parables, using the prophet's name
To make me feel guilty; the real shame

Is quoting God's creation in this way –
It's sacrilege and for this you will pay!"

The husband, whom her words had stung,
replied,
"Your features are Avarice, you can't hide

Behind rhetoric. This bare way of life
Should bring harmony to a man and wife.

You call me the snake and its charmer too:
Have you considered that applies to you?

Believe me, I lack nothing, we are blessed
With all that God gives us as he knows best.

The child who plays at going round and round
Imagines he is on the spinning ground.

And just so, it's ego that falsifies
And turns the light of Truth into dark Lies.

Patience will grant you glimpses of
God's light. . . ."
And thus they argued through the day
and night.

THE GREENGROCER AND
THE PARROT

A greengrocer had a pet singing bird
Whose dulcet tones all the neighbourhood
heard.

This parrot would even sometimes take charge
Speaking to the customers, by and large

In dialects in which she was well-versed
And sing in parrot melodies she'd rehearsed.

One day fluttering up through the shop's air
She knocked some rose-oil bottles everywhere.

The greengrocer came back to his shop and saw
The spillage of the rose-oil on the floor

And concluding that his stock was thus defiled
The parrot's master went utterly wild.

He grabbed the bird with savage hands
and mauled
Her, pulling off her feathers leaving her bald.

The parrot then fell silent, not a squawk
Escaped her beak, she wouldn't sing or talk.

The greengrocer was maddened with remorse.
"Why in God's name did I resort to force?

And violence against my pet, my joy
I would pay any pir, I would employ

Any means to restore my bird's speech" –
He begged his bird for just one squawk
or screech.

The days passed in this silence which
they shared;
The bird was dumb, the greengrocer despaired

Until one day a mendicant passed by
Completely bald and hairless as the sky

Our unfeathered parrot began to squawk
Seeming suddenly inspired to talk.

"Hey baldy!" she shouted to the shaven man,
"Did you crash bottles or kick over a can?"

The customers laughed at this cute comment
The poor bird thought that all baldness
was sent

As punishment for any who spill oil
Judging this dervish through her own turmoil.

THE DERVISH AT THE DOOR

A dervish knocked at a rich household door
And begged for a slice of bread.
"I don't care if it's fresh or stale,"
The hungry mendicant said.

"This isn't a bloody bakery!"
The man of the house replied.
"Some left-over gristle or fat will do,"
Said the dervish swallowing his pride.

" You mistake my house for a butchery,"
(This home owner was rude)
"I'm sorry, a cup of water will do,
I'm content to go without food."

Whatever the Dervish asked for
The man dismissed. One could tell
How nasty he was, when he begged a drink
He asked, "You think I own a free well?"

The dervish, hurt, ran into the house
And lifted his robe as to relieve
Himself, when the householder cried
"How dare you try this, get out, leave!"

The dervish said, "You call this home?
I can see no human lives here.
This is open desert where creatures roam
And I can relieve myself without fear

Of indecency." He continued,
"You are no falcon on a royal wrist
Or much of a peacock, your colours are pale
You're not even a parrot as parrots insist

On speaking like humans they imitate.
You're not like the Hoopoe whom Solomon met
And sent with a message to Sheba's court.
Or even a thrush with songs of regret.

What manner of creature are you then,
Who would turn a poor beggar from
	your door?
With hoarded possessions for yourself
I asked you for water, nothing more

And you with your rudeness turned me away
That's turning your back on the Supreme One
Who taught us to shun all earthly wealth
And live as meek of the earth have done.

THE GNATS AND SOLOMON

A swarm of gnats appeared at Suleiman's court.
The King of Justice asked them what
they sought.

"You are, O king, defender of the weak!
There's none weaker than us - that's why
we seek

Justice through you." The king then asked
these gnats,
"Who is your complaint against, because that's

The rule of justice which allows defence
From those who are accused of some offence."

The gnats agreed and named their oppressor
As the world's winds which whirl and sweep
and whirr

Through their habitat, stirring up the grass.
The King said, "Very well, before I pass

Any judgement, I must hear the Winds' case.
So courtiers, bring the East Wind to this place."

The east Wind had no choice but to obey
And arriving there, blew the gnats away.

Such is the fate of seekers who complain
When God arrives to alleviate their pain.

They aren't taken by force and swept aside
But like the gnats and wind, they're unified.

THE CALIPH AND THE
CONCUBINE

The Caliph of Egypt was told
Mosul's King had a concubine
Whose beauty was so startling that
Men who had eyes and hearts would pine

For a favour from this maiden.
The Caliph's informer then drew
A likeness of this fair vision
On paper which instantly threw

The Caliph into the firm grip
Of fascination and of lust.
He sent for his army command
Saying, "Go to Mosul, I must

Possess this girl at any cost."
The Captain in charge of the force
Laid siege for a week to Mosul
With his army and in the course

Of battle routing the defence.
Mosul's King said he'd surrender -
He wanted to stop the killing
And even agreed to render

The city to Egypt's Caliph.
"I'll give him everything that's mine."
The Captain sent this message back:
"All he wants is your concubine."

The King of Mosul was relieved.
"The eunuchs shall deliver her.
Tell the Caliph I'll gladly send
This idol to her worshipper."

This poor girl was delivered
Into the Caliph's Captain's charge
And as soon as he glanced at her
Some thoughts he couldn't camouflage

Rushed into his mind. Was it love
Or was it lust that overcame
The Captain? This wild emotion
Is universal so no blame

Accrued to him or any man
Who feels compelled by Adam's urge –
The force that turns the earth to plants
From which then animals emerge.

The Captain now restrains himself
But obsessed in his sleep it seems
He's making frantic love to her
In throes of ecstatic wet dreams.

At dawn the Captain wakes to find
That this lover was never there,
That he had a fantastic dream
And spurted semen in the air.

But his obsession didn't go;
It was so strong he would defy
The Caliph's orders though he knew
He could then be sentenced to die

For this folly that we call love.
So did this captain act in haste
When he cast discretion aside
And of that nectar took a taste?

Our wild fantasy can construct
A phantom in a well that grows
And confronting a lion's pride
Conquers them one by one and throws

Them in that well. Take care and don't
Trust men with women in your care
As passions, like cotton and flint
Can suddenly flash and flare.

This Captain feels he can't return
As he was ordered, right away
Instead he camps in a meadow
Feeling this compulsion to stray.

His reason is completely blind,
His head filled with a drumming sound.
He's so compelled by this passion
He can't tell open sky from ground

So, approaching this maiden he
Strips her and takes her to his bed
And just as his erect penis
Is poised to take her maidenhead

He hears a tumult in the camp
And shouts and screams outside the tent.
So, springing up naked he grabs
The nearest sharp instrument

And rushing out bravely confronts
A black lion on the attack,
And with a single mighty blow
His scimitar descends to crack

The lion's skull from head to jaw.
And having won this victory
He rushes back into the tent
Desperate to make love and she,

Seeing that throughout all this time
He's maintained his virility
She's flattered and they make wild love
In hot entwining unity.

When two lovers start to fuck
And lose themselves in love's embrace
An unseen third spirit enters,
A spirit with a hidden face.

Since Adam and Eve such union
Results in generations born
That spirit then becomes new flesh
And from the cradling womb is torn

To exist and to grow and speak
Manifestation of that tense
Moment when the child was conceived
When man and woman merge all sense

And in that coupling are as one.

The captain lost in this affair,
Like a gnat drowned in buttermilk
Of such spirits was unaware

And so suddenly snapping out
Of the spell he then turned to her,
"Don't ever say a word of this
To the caliph or else I fear

For both our lives". With this caution
He brought his love to Egypt and
To the caliph who was entranced
Saying he couldn't understand

How she in the flesh seemed even
More beautiful, a hundred-fold
Than the portrait that he had seen
Or things about her he'd been told.

A pupil asked his wise teacher,
"Are false and true together one?"
The teacher said, "For example
It's false that bats flee from the sun.

What's true," the teacher continued,
"Is bats flee from the idea
In their minds of the blazing sun
And shelter in their caves for fear

Of the perception of the mind.
Your idea of an enemy
Makes you seek out specific friends
And keep protective company.

Moosa with revealed inner light
Can illuminate Mount Sinai
But when he descends to the plains
The light he brings will fade and die.

The murals painted on the walls
Of bathhouses are of great wars.
Remember as you view these deeds
That painted courage is not yours!

Can sounds heard by human ears
Be transformed into rays of light,
Uniting both your eye and ear
And making hearing sharp as sight?

Your body then can mirror rays
Reflecting sights your ear recovers
And sound now parallel to sight
Guides the lonely to their lovers."

The Caliph coming face to face
Suffered a flash, blinding lightning!
Egypt, his kingdom disappeared
In that flash he lost everything

He had possessed; he could now see
That possession was vanity;
Like passing breath through a moustache
All substance is insanity.

The atheists and skeptics say
"Death is the end - life doesn't last;
There are no other dimensions
Beyond this present and this past!"

But just because a little child
Lives partly in fantasy
And partly in the real world
Doesn't mean rationality

Has abandoned all human minds.
And just because some may deny
The presence of a Divine Love
Won't make it withdraw like a shy

Bride blushing at her bridegroom's door.
Yusuf's brothers could never see
The future that his father knew
Would be the gift of prophecy.

And Moosa at first only saw
A stick that was a piece of wood
Which through his inner eye became
A viper with a cobra's hood.

The infinite is all around.
The foolish say they stick to facts
The only ones these Skeptics know
Are genitals and digestive tracts.

So, let the fools and skeptics say
That God the Friend does not exist
Don't linger listening to them,
The ramblings of the atheist.

The Caliph now consumed by lust
With his penis hard and ready
Approached this captive maiden
Anticipating a heady

Encounter in such abandon
In hours and hours of pure delight.
But as he tried to hold her close
There came a warning in the night.

It was just a tiny sound
The scrambling that a mouse might make.
The Caliph turned in abject fear
Thinking the scrambling was a snake.

He jumps up, leaving the girl in bed.
His penis now begins to droop.
The poor girl as she looks on
Lets out a loud triumphant whoop -

She laughs out loud at what she sees.
The Captain's penis comes to mind
Stiff even while killing the beast.
She knew she was being unkind,

Mocking the prurient Caliph.
Of this defiance she was proud
And pointing at his hairy crotch
She shrieked with laughter. With a loud

Hoot she derided the Caliph
Who was furious and drew his sword.
"Tell me the truth; what makes you laugh?
I can read minds, you can't afford

To lie to me. I have to know
The whole truth or I'll strike you dead.
You've hurt me and this sword is sharp
I swear I will chop off your head.

To substantiate this like threat
He piled six Quran's in a stack
And swearing on them vowed to kill
This girl who was taken aback.

But suppressing her terror now
She recounted in great detail
The camp, the Captain's tent and how
He had ventured out to assail

And kill the lion while he stood
As naked as when he was born
And then his return to the tent
His prick hard as a rhino's horn.

And as spoke she contrasted
The Caliph's trepid impotence
At a small mouse's scampering.
And suddenly her words made sense

As if hidden things came to light.
Every bad seed that mortals sow
Will, nourished by sun and rain,
Push through the earth and wildly grow

Without blossoms or fruit or grain.
In spring the secrets of the earth
From earth's lips sprout stalks, stems
and leaves
– Proof of the resurrected birth.

Causes can never resemble
Their effects or the things they breed.
The spindly vine grows the round grape;
No blossom resembles a seed.

The good book says that Issah was
Born of the breath of Jibraeel.
Yet Issah took on human form
And just so effects can conceal

The secrets of their origins.
We suffer in body and brain
Asking the unanswered question:
Who know the cause of human pain?

The caliph now relenting says,
"I took this girl in lust and pride
Not asking whom she loved nor why
A love she had promised to hide.

Then like a sign the mouse appeared
To prove I couldn't take by force
By rendering me impotent
Preventing this vain intercourse.

This treachery would have turned one
Trusted friend into a traitor,
So first I'll make a proposal
And ask you then, which is greater."

The caliph said, "Go back to him.
Tell him my wives won't let me add
Another one to my harem
And please convey to him I'm glad

He brought you from Mosul and so
He shall in marriage have your hand
And I, the Caliph shall declare
A holiday in all the land.

Nobility requires the strength
To leave indulgences behind
And end cycles of secret lust
Which bedevil all mankind.

The Captain's loving may be an
Admirable ability,
It's but the husk; the precious grain
Is that Caliph's nobility.

FIRE IN MEDINA

In the time of caliph Omar
A fire engulfed Medina
And burnt every building of
The city, sparing not a spar

Or beam of wood or brick or stone
And spread then to the city's trees.
The monstrous blaze even consumed
The nests of birds and hives of bees.

The waters of the city's baths
Got heated and began to boil;
The fire began to consume
The Oases and scorch the soil.

The citizens of Medina
Brought water and poured vinegar
On the flames which kept spreading as
Though impelled by some sinister

Forces beyond plain combustion.
The people then approached Omar
Saying, "This fire won't be doused
Please tell us how to quell it, Sir!"

Omar said, "It's a sign from God,
A punishment for stinginess.
You pour water and vinegar
But give no wealth that you possess

To those in need." These people said
"We have supported charity
And given as prescribed." Omar
Said, "Yes you have done your duty

As the book and tradition say
But prescriptions don't open hearts.
When you give what you can't afford
To give, that's where charity starts."

Omar said, "Don't let charity
Be a badge of your social pride
Don't be philanthropic to claim
That you are on pure virtue's side.

Don't arm the criminals with swords
And shun the vulgar and uncouth;
Seek out the faithful and keep faith
With the companions of the truth."

THE LAZIEST

A merchant who had three sons specified
On his deathbed his will and testament.
His sons stood round reserving their lament
As he spoke his last words before he died.

He said the town's judge would have to decide
Which of his three sons was the laziest..
He specified they all should pass a test
And that his will was never to divide

His fortune equally among these boys –
The laziest of them should take it all.
The old man was cunning as a jackal –
This 'laziness' was the best of his ploys

To find out which son had a mystic gift.
Just as the mystic lets God sow the seeds,
Knowing his harvest will provide our needs,
This test was just a way the judge could sift

The chaff of the practical from the grain
Of mystical accord. He asked each son
To pass the test of voices: every one
Reveals an inner self, their joy and pain.

The breeze crossing a garden of roses
And that crossing an ash heap will convey
Distinct odours they picked up on their way.
The lion's roar and the wolf's howl exposes

Their different inner selves. A cooking pot
Gives off odours of sweet and sour stew
Or of stale meat cooked in a heady brew.
So, the judge applied the test and asked what

They could tell of a person from their speech,
The eldest said, "The timbre of his voice
Will tell me all. If he's silent by choice
I'll know him through intuition as each

Person's silence vibrates in my mind."
The second son said, "I would make him say
Something in answer, asking if I may
Do this or that, something cruel or kind

That would force him to speak!" "But just
suppose,"
The judge said, "that he knows that it's a ploy
And so he remains reticent and coy?
Like the mother who tells a child who goes
Through a graveyard that if he sees a ghost
He should run at it to scare it away.
Then suppose the child interrupts her to say
"Don't ghosts have mothers?" — his cheeky
riposte -

"Who's told the ghost that he must do the same
And if he runs at me I'll disappear?"

The judge concluded now that it was clear
This second son had forfeited his claim

To the inheritance. And now the third
Son was asked how he'd venture to engage
Someone who wouldn't speak and how he'd
gauge
The inner being of one he had not heard.

He answered, "I'd sit in silence before
This silent man and conspire to pour
Through this silence that we seem to endure
A language beyond joy or grief, a pure

Transmission to see if his soul is bright
And if a window opens when I speak,

And through that window both our beings seek
To endow mutual silence with insight."

Thus inaction, through action of the mind
Convinced the judge that their father's
will meant
His wealth was only mystical ascent
And that 'laziness' should be redefined.

TATTOOING

In Qazwin they believe tattoos
Of any images they choose

Can bring them luck and change their fate
And through their magic recreate

Their spirit and their character.
So one, approaching a barber,

Asks for one on his shoulder blade
In blue ink and whatever shade

Would represent the most fierce
Lion. "Let the needle pierce

My muscles so that this image
Copies the King of Beast's visage."

The barber started with the blue
-Inked needle. The first prick drew

From this patient a howl of pain.
"This is like torture! Please restrain

The way your needle pricks my skin;
Which bit are you tattooing in?"

The barber answered, "It's the tail,
The swishing symbol of the male

Animal." The customer said,
"Please do some other bit instead."

The barber silently concurs,
Starting to now tattoo the ears.

The patient then began to shout,
"Please leave both these wretched ears out!"

And as the barber shaped the mane
This customer screams out in pain

Saying, "Please can't this lion be
Bereft of such anatomy?"

The barber dropped his needle and,
Saying he couldn't understand

How a lion could be portrayed
Without the body nature made.

And so my friend, withstand all pain.
Let no impulse triumph again.

THE EVIDENCE OF BREATH

Kind Reader, before your hand turns this page
Please hear the story of the Indian sage

Who met a group of pilgrims on the road
Who were tired and hungry. He bestowed

Upon them understanding, knowing they
Would eat any creature who came their way!

The sage said, "Pilgrims, please heed my advice.
I know the hungry will pay any price

To get some stuff into their flat bellies
But I beseech you, listen to me please.

You'll pass through jungles some miles down
the road
Which are well-known as elephants' abode.

You'll find plump young elephant herds
will cross
Your path. They're young and playful and
they toss

Sticks and mangoes in their playful mood
At travellers, but please don't think it rude -

These young tuskers think of humans as friends
And normally an older one attends

To these young herds. But as I came away
The trees beside my path began to sway

I then heard a trumpeting of distress
It was quite frightening, I must confess.

The sound came from a female elephant.
The swaying trees I'd seen had felt the brunt

Of her frustration. I guessed she had lost
Her young ones in the jungle. Now she tossed

The trees she had uprooted in her pain;
She'd searched three days and nights but
all in vain."

And saying this he added some advice,
"Heed what I say or you will pay the price.

I see you're desperately hungry but
Don't be ruled by the longings of your gut

Or by your palette's overwhelming greed.
This jungle's trees bear all the fruit you need.

Be warned, don't seek the flesh of elephants;
It will cause you deep and fatal penance."

The sage departed; the pilgrims moved on
And soon to their surprise they came upon

A baby elephant a few days old
Asleep on a bed of leaves. They got hold

Of this poor creature and they lit a fire.
One of their group reminded them of the dire

Consequences the sage had predicted.
The rest ignored his entreaties and did

Precisely what they were told would tempt fate.
They choked and roasted the infant and ate

Its flesh and when they'd finished fell asleep.
The one who hadn't eaten said he'd keep

A watch on their belongings through the night.
He was awake when in the dim moonlight

A crashing through the jungle could be heard
And the huge mother elephant appeared.

She put her trunk to this guard's lips to smell
His mouth's and gut's odours as she could tell

Which of these beasts had devoured her
poor child?
The breath of the innocent one was mild,

Flavoured with the berries he'd had that day
So, leaving him and still seeking her prey

She smelt the breath of those who were asleep
And though what she detected made her weep

She flung each guilty one into the air
Crushing their bones, killing them then
and there!

The young in innocence will always stray,
Though saints and prophets have showed them
the way

All pride, greed and concupiscence will show
Up in the words you use – and those who know

Can detect the odours of that within.
And though you say a prayer to hide a sin

If you've eaten onions the odour will
Pervade your breath and no protest can kill

The evidence that rides upon the air
And betrays you – so liars all beware!

PATIENCE

The artist and the craftsman are a pair
Whose skills can fill the void of what's
not there

A builder patches a wall's crumbling hole
The Saki fills the tavern's empty bowl

The painter brush paints scenes not seen before
The carpenter gives entrances a door

Endeavour looks for emptiness to fill
All emptiness is only such until

Those who confront the vast nothing inside
Themselves invite the unseen Ocean's tide.

We label our future's emptiness "death"
Though from it we've been granted life
and breath

God allows this reversal to occur
We desire the viper's pit and fear

The safe and beautiful expanse around
It. The same moral message can be found

In Attar's story of the Hindu boy
Captured by King Mahmud's troops to enjoy

And indulge nasty, lustful tendencies
Though Mahmud's intentions were pure
as breeze.

And leaving the loot and spoils to the rest
He took the boy to his fatherly breast

Adopting him as an anointed son
Nominating him as the chosen one

Treating him as in every way his own
Flesh and blood, placing him on a gold throne.

But as he did the boy started to cry
So, a perplexed Mahmud asked the poor
boy why?

The boy said that he remembered that his dad
And mum would take King Mahmud's name
and add

That he would on one of his Indian raids
Carry away naughty boys and young maids

And use them then as slaves. Who would have
thought
I'd be sitting by you, a Prince in court."

The meaning of this story should be clear
That change of any kind is our worst fear

The Hindu boy is Everyman, no less
And Mahmud's is our spirit's emptiness

The mother and father are Attachment
To blood, habits and comforts which were sent

To imprison you rather than protect
The fear of emptiness makes you reject

The prospect of finding joy in that court
And shedding tears of delight at the thought

Of those mistaken parents and their threat.
You'll embrace the unknown without regret.

Your body, like an armour chain-mail vest
Put's your soul's temperature to the test

Too cold in winter and then much too hot
In summer. Or think of the garden plot

In which a rose blossoms next to a thorn
The portrait of all beauty's Patience born

To nurse an infant camel for three years.
In friendship this Patience always appears

Consistency and Patience are the way
So dissolve in that Emptiness and say

"These things that come and go are not for me
Rising and setting is inconstancy!".
Or else you'll be the campfire which must
Flare by the roadside and then turn to dust.

SONG OF THE REED

O let the grieving of the reed be heard;
It sings of the parting it has suffered.

"I was from the bed of reeds rudely rent
O humans resonate in my lament.

To the breast that has suffered separation
This cry of parting is a sad libation.

The one who finds himself so far from home
Thinks only of the day he will come home

I wandered in gatherings of men who
Were sorrowful though some were happy too

And though from among those I made the best
Of friends I kept my secret in my breast.

My secret is the essence of this grief
To which no sight or sound can bring relief."

Our bodies give our souls a sanctuary
And yet the soul remains a mystery.

The flute's music is not man's breath, but fire
This fire is love, the essence of desire

The turbulence of love is in the wine
Those not on fire will never know love divine.

The reed is the voice of all who are lovelorn;
Its melodies ensure all veils are torn.

All opposites are One, disease and cure.
Is the reed's longing for pure love impure?

The reed sings the song that broke
Majnu's heart
The song of belonging and being torn apart

The sense is senseless to all that has occurred
The sensitive ear is receptive to the word.

Through worldly attachments the days turn
into nights
Rendering as longings all our appetites.

Though time makes the ages, don't fear
getting old,
Let all that is Holy, before your eyes unfold.

The fish that's born to water needn't fear
a flood;

For the hungry human, weakness thins
the blood.

Raw meat can't predict the taste of
cooked sauce
So farewell — that's the end of this